A-Lev

Revision Cards

AQA Year 1 and AS

New Syllabus 2015

Dr C. Boes

Condensed Revision Cards/Notes for a
Successful Exam Preparation

Designed to Facilitate Memorization

www.alevelchemistryrevision.co.uk

Text copyright © 2015 Dr. Christoph Boes

All rights reserved

Cover Image from Kodak EasyShare Picture Gallery

All other Images copyright © 2015 Dr. Christoph Boes

Self-published 2015

ISBN-13: 9781517435080

ISBN-10: 1517435080

How to use these notes

Revision notes (revision cards) are an effective and successful way to prepare for exams. They contain the necessary exam knowledge in a condensed, easy to memorize form. These notes are designed for the final stage of revision and require a thorough understanding of the topics. If this understanding is lacking then help from a professional tutor and additional studies of text books or revision guides is suggested.

This is the print version of the eBook, which is available in Amazon's Kindle store. To keep the price low this paper copy has been published in black and white. The corresponding eBook contains coloured illustrations.

These revision notes are organized in different chapters according to the new 2015 AQA Year 1 & AS syllabus. Each chapter contains individual revision cards covering all the necessary topics. Everything in *italic* is optional knowledge, aimed at students who want to excel or want to continue with A2. **Bold** labels important keywords or key definitions. 'data sheet' indicates information which will be provided on the data sheet during the exam and does not need to be memorized. Exam-specific tips are highlighted in grey.

How to memorize: - The revision cards are introduced by their titles on a separate page. After reading the title you should try to write down the content of the card without looking at the next page. Write down everything you remember, even if you are not sure. Then check if your answers are correct; if not rewrite the incorrect ones.

At the beginning when you are still unfamiliar with the cards, it might help to read them a few times first. If they contain a lot of content you can cover the revision card with a piece of paper and slowly reveal the header and sub content. While you uncover it try to remember what is written in the covered part, e.g. the definition for a term you just uncovered. This uncovering technique is for the early stage, later you should be able to write down the whole content after just reading the header. If this is the case, move to the next card. If not bookmark the card and memorize it repeatedly. Do three to four sessions per week until you know all the cards of one chapter word-perfectly. Then move on to the next section.

An even better memorization option is to ask somebody to check your knowledge by reading the header aloud and comparing your answer to the content. Alternatively, get together in learning groups and support each other. Make it a game to check your knowledge by creating questions and compete as groups like in a pub quiz. Discuss questions which you don't understand; your friend might know the answers or ask your teacher or tutor. More tips about memorization techniques and how to prepare for exams can be found on my website: http://www.alevelchemistryrevision.co.uk/

Contents

Unit 1 – Foundation Chemistry

1.1 Atomic Structure

Basic Definitions

Basic Definitions

Atom: smallest unit of an element
-> consist of electrons organized in orbitals/shells and a nucleus made from protons and neutrons

Subatomic Particle	Relative mass	Charge
Proton	1	+1
Neutron	1	0
Electron	1/2000	-1

Element: same kind of atoms (same atomic number)

Isotopes: atoms with same number of protons but different number of neutrons *(same element: same atomic number but different mass number)*

Atomic number: number of protons

Mass number: protons + neutrons

Ion: charged particle (positive-> **cation**, negative -> **anion**)

Electron Configuration

Electron Configuration

Orbital: Region of space in which **electrons** are most **likely to be found**. One orbital contains maximum **two electrons**, which must have **opposite spins**.
- Orbitals of the same subshell are filled individually first
- 4s get filled and emptied before 3d (see revision card 'Transition metals')

N: $1s^2 2s^2 2p^3$ [He] $2s^2 2p^3$

> **2: shell**
> **p: subshell**
> **3: number of electrons (in subshell)**

Box diagram:

Electronic configuration of N

Energy

2p³ | ↑ | ↑ | ↑ |

2s² | ↑↓ |

1s² | ↑↓ |

Shapes of orbitals:

s-orbital: p-orbital:

Sphere   Dumbbell

Subshells	Orbitals	Electrons
s	1	2
p	3	6
d	5	10
f	7	14

Number of electrons per shell (n): $2n^2$

1.2 Amount of Substance

Relative Atomic mass - Definitions

Relative Atomic mass - Definitions

Relative Atomic mass A_r
Is the average (weighted) mass of an element's isotopes relative to 1/12 the mass of a ^{12}C atom [no unit]

$$A_r = \frac{(a\% \times A_1) + (b\% \times A_2)}{100}$$

a%:   percentage of Isotope 1
b%:   percentage of Isotope 2
A_1:   Relative Isotopic mass of Isotope 1
A_2:   Relative Isotopic mass of Isotope 2

=> A_r and **Relative Isotopic Abundance** can be worked out from a Mass Spectrum (a%, b% from y-axis of each peak) -> see revision card 'Mass spectrometry' 2.11

Relative isotopic mass
Is the mass of an atom of an isotope relative to 1/12 the mass of a ^{12}C atom [no unit]

Molar mass M
Mass of one mole of a substance [g mol^{-1}]

Relative molecular Mass M_r (relative formula mass)
of a compound is the sum of the relative atomic masses of all its atoms. [no unit]

Mole

Mole

1 mole = 6.02 x 10²³ (Avogadro's number N_A -> data sheet)

Definition: number of atoms in 12 g of ^{12}C

$$n = \frac{m}{M}$$

n: number of moles [moles]
m: mass [g]
M_r: molar mass [g/mol]
[ ]:   units

$$N = n \times N_A$$

N: number of particles [no unit]
N_A: Avogardro's number 6.02 x 10²³ [mol⁻¹]

Molar Gas Volume

Molar Gas Volume

Volume of 1 mole of any gas = 24 dm^3 at standard conditions (data sheet)

Standard conditions: 298 K (25 C), 101.3 kPa

$$V_x = n \text{ x } 24 \text{ dm}^3 \text{mol}^{-1}$$

V_x: unknown volume [dm^3]
n: number of moles [moles]

Converting cm^3 into dm^3

$$x \text{ cm}^3 = \frac{x}{1000} \text{ dm}^3$$

Ideal gas equation:

$$pV = nRT$$

p: pressure **[Pa]**
V: volume **[m^3]**
R: 8.31 J K^{-1} mol^{-1} (gas constant -> data sheet)
T: temperature **[K]**   (0 C = 273 K)

-> make sure you are using correct SI units - see [ ]

Empirical and Molecular Formulae

Empirical and Molecular Formulae

Molecular formula: actual number of atoms in a molecule e. g. Ethene C_2H_4, O_2
=> closer to reality, generally used in equations.

Empirical formula: smallest whole number ratio of atoms in a compound e. g . CH_2 or O
=> Empirical formula is used when trying to find out the molecular formula of an unknown organic compound by burning it (elemental analysis)

- For salts: chemical formula identical with empirical formula
- For Molecules: Molecular formula is a multiple of empirical formula

How to work out empirical formulae from grams (experiment – burning hydrocarbon):
- Use n=m/M to calculate moles of each element (take mole ratios into account e.g. H in H_2O 2 : 1)
- Divide by smallest mole number to get ratio (empirical formula)

How to work out empirical formulae from percentages:
- Set 100 % as 100 g, then same as above ('How to work out empirical formulae from grams')

How to work out molecular formulae from empirical formulae and molecular mass
- Divide Molecular mass by empirical mass -> factor
- Multiply empirical formula with factor -> molecular formula

Example calculations – Empirical and Molecular formulae

Example calculations – Empirical and Molecular formulae

When an unknown hydrocarbon with Mr = 70 g/mol is burnt in excess oxygen, we get 6.6 g of CO_2 and 2.7 g of H_2O (elemental analysis).

What is the empirical and molecular formula of this compound?

Calculate empirical formula first

Moles CO_2 :
n = 6.6 g/44 g/mol = 0.15 mol (1 mole C in 1 mole CO_2 -> factor 1)
=> Moles C: n = 0.15 mol

Moles H_2O:
n = 2.7 g/18 g/mol = 0.15 mol (2 moles H in 1 mole H_2O -> factor 2)
=> Moles H: n = 2 x 0.15 mol = 0.3 mol

Divide by smallest mole number:
C 0.15/0.15 = **1**, H 0.3/0.15 = **2**
Ratio   C : H   **1 : 2**
Empirical formula: C_1H_2 => CH_2

Calculate Molecular formula from Mr and empirical formula

Unknown hydrocarbon	Mr = 70 g/mol
Empirical mass CH_2	Mr = 14 g/mol
Factor:	70 g/mol / 14 g/mol = 5
Molecular formula:	5 x CH_2 => C_5H_{10}

=> Unknown Hydrocarbon was Pentene

Mole equations – calculate masses

Mole equations – calculate masses

1) Calculate moles for given compound by using $n = m/M$
2) Circle or highlight mole numbers in front of related compounds (given and unknown)
3) Determine mole ratio for unknown compound
4) Get mole factor by dividing both mole numbers so that known compound becomes 1
5) Multiply moles of given compound with factor to get moles of unknown compound
6) Calculate mass of unknown compound by using $n = m/M$
7) Do not round whilst still calculating. Carry as many digits through the calculation as possible (at least 3) until you reach the final answer.
8) Write the answer with the appropriate number of significant figures: if the data are given in 3 significant figures then the answer should also be given in 3 significant figures (see below)
9) If the last non-significant figure is 1 - 4 round down, if 5 – 9 round up.

Example:

Calculate amount of O_2 (in grams) produced if 3.24 g of iron (III) nitrate is heated

$$4 \ Fe(NO_3)_3 \rightarrow 2Fe_2O_3 + 12NO_2 + 3 \ O_2$$

1) Moles $Fe(NO_3)_3$: $n = 3.24$ g/ 241.8 g/mol = 0.0134 moles
2) See mole equation above
3) Ratio: 3 : 4
4) Factor for O_2: ¾ = 0.75 ($Fe(NO_3)_3$: 4/4 = 1)
5) Moles O_2 : 0.75 x 0.0134 moles = 0.0100 moles
6) Mass O_2: $m = n \ x \ M = 0.0100$ mol x 32 g/mol = 0.322 g

Concentration

Concentration

Mole concentration:

$$c = \frac{n}{V}$$

n: moles [mol]
V: volume [dm^3]
c: concentration [mol dm^{-3}]

1 dm^3 = 1000 cm^3

Mass concentration:

$$c = \frac{m}{V}$$

m: mass [g]
c: concentration [g dm^{-3}]

Percentage yield & Atom economy

Percentage yield

percentage yield $=$ $\dfrac{\textbf{actual yield}}{\textbf{theoretical yield}}$ **x 100**

units of actual/theoretical yield (of products): [grams] or [moles]

Reasons for loss:
- Reaction not complete (clumps instead of powder)
- Loss of product (sticking to vessel, evaporation of liquids)
- By-products
- Impurities of reactants

Atom economy

% atom economy $=$ $\dfrac{\textbf{M}_r \textbf{ desired product}}{\textbf{ΣM}_r \textbf{ all products}}$ **x 100**

-> 100 % for addition reactions

Benefits of high atom economy
- Environmental and economic benefits
- Avoiding waste
- Reduces separation costs
- High sustainability (less raw material)
- High efficiency

Example calculation

$(NH_4)_2SO_{4(s)} + 2NaOH_{(aq)} \rightarrow 2NH_{3(g)} + Na_2SO_{4(aq)} + 2H_2O_{(l)}$

Calculate the percentage atom economy for the production of ammonia.

% atom economy $=$ $\dfrac{2 \times 17}{2 \times 17 + 142 + 2 \times 18}$ x 100

$=$ 16.0 %

Ionic equations

Ionic equations

Spectator Ions: ions which do not take part in the reaction

They can be removed from the full equation to give an ionic equation

Full equation:

$Cl_2 + 2NaBr \rightarrow Br_2 + 2NaCl$

0   +1 -1   0   +1 -1

Na^+ does not change oxidation states -> spectator ion, can be removed from equation =>

Ionic equation:

$Cl_2 + 2Br^- \rightarrow Br_2 + 2Cl^-$

0   -1   0   -1

1.3 Bonding

Ionic and Covalent Compounds & Bonds

Ionic and Covalent Compounds & Bonds

Compound: atoms of different elements bonded together

Salts - Ionic compounds: Metal/Non metal
-> consists of ions ('Dot-and Cross' diagram: square bracket with charge around ion)
-> forms lattice with alternating charges
Chemical formula gives ratio
Physical properties:
- high melting points
- soluble in water
- conduct electricity in solution or when molten
Examples: $NaCl$, $MgCl_2$

Ionic bond: electrostatic attraction between oppositely charged ions

Na^+ Cl^- Na^+ Cl^- Na^+ Cl^-
Cl^- Na^+ Cl^- Na^+ Cl^- Na^+
Na^+ Cl^- Na^+ Cl^- Na^+ Cl^-
Cl^- Na^+ Cl^- Na^+ Cl^- Na^+

Molecules - Covalent compounds: Non metals
-> Collection of atoms ('Dot-and-Cross' diagram: overlapping circles for bonds)
-> Different shapes
Chemical formula tells which atoms are directly connected with each other
Physical properties:
- low melting point,
- not soluble in water,
- not conducting electricity
Examples CH_4, H_2O

Covalent bond: sharing **a pair** of electrons

Dative covalent bond: both electrons of the covalent bond come from **one** atom (**arrow** instead of dash) e. g. NH_4^+

Shapes of molecules I

Shapes of molecules

Valence shell Electron-Pair Repulsion Theory:
- Negative charges of electron pairs in covalent bonds **repel** each other
- Lone pairs of electrons repel more (closer to central atom) => smaller bond angle
- Shape depends on **number of charge clouds** (bonds, electron pairs)

One central atom with 2 partners (charge clouds):

=> linear, 180 , CO_2

One central atom with 3 partners:

=> trigonal planar, 120 , BF_3

One central atom with 4 partners:

=> tetrahedral, 109.5, CH_4, NH_4^+ (draw straight-line-bonds next to each other)

One central atom with 3 partners & 1 lone pair of electrons:

=> trigonal pyramidal, 107°, NH_3, SO_3^{2-}

Shapes of molecules II

One central atom with 2 partners & 2 lone pair of electrons:

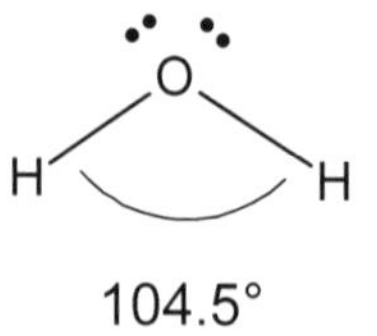

104.5°

=> bent/non-linear, 104.5°, H_2O

One central atom with 5 partners

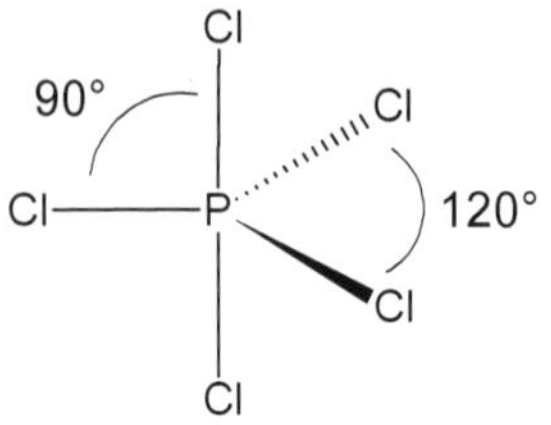

=> trigonal bipyramidal, 120° & 90°, PCl_5

One central atom with 6 partners:

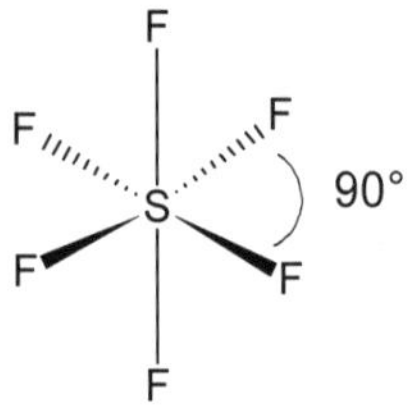

=> octahedral, 90°, SF_6

To get other examples: use a different element from the same group as the central atom and keep same partners

Electronegativity

Electronegativity

Definition: ability of an atom to attract electrons in a covalent bond

-> Increases across period (more protons)
-> Decreases down group:
- more shells, more distance
- more shielding,
- despite more protons

-> Fluorine most electronegative element (then O_2, then Cl_2)
-> Elements closer to F: more electronegative
-> large differences in electronegativity result in ionic compounds
-> small differences result in covalent compounds

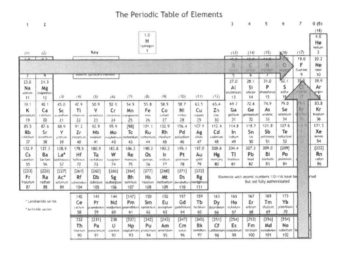

The Periodic Table of Elements

Intermolecular forces

Intermolecular forces

keep molecules together => model to explain physical state (melting, boiling point)

1) Permanent dipole-dipole interactions
Permanent dipole contains **polar bonds** due to different **electronegativities** (-> shift in electron density)

$\delta+$ $\delta-$

H - Cl

δ means slightly (or partially)

Molecules with polar bonds can be permanent dipoles

2) Instantaneous dipole–induced dipole interactions (Van der Waals)
Non-polar molecules contain **non polar bonds** (equal electronegativities like Cl_2)

Temporary/instantaneous dipole
-> Electron cloud moving randomly (uneven distribution)
- depends on number of electrons and surface area (points of contact)
- weakest intermolecular force

Induced dipole
Permanent dipole or instantaneous dipole can induce dipoles in non-polar molecules

e.g. mixture of HCl and Cl_2

3) Hydrogen Bonds
O, F, N with an H bonded directly to these atoms (-NH_2, -OH, HF)
- Hydrogen atom flips between two partners (special type of covalent bond)
- 5 – 10 % of the strength of a normal covalent bond, but strongest intermolecular force
- Draw with dotted line between H and lone pair of electrons:

$$\delta+ \quad \delta- \qquad \delta+ \quad \delta- \qquad \delta+ \quad \delta-$$
$$H - \ddot{\underset{\cdot\cdot}{F}} : \cdots\cdots H - \ddot{\underset{\cdot\cdot}{F}} : \cdots\cdots H - \ddot{\underset{\cdot\cdot}{F}} :$$

Anomalous properties of water
-> high boiling point
-> lower density of ice because of more H-bonds than liquid water

Metallic bonding

Metallic bonding

Def.: Electrostatic attraction between metal **cations** and **delocalized electrons** from the outer shell (**sea of electrons**)

Across period higher melting point:
- charges of cations increase: Na^+, Mg^{2+}, Al^{3+}
- more delocalized electrons (negative charges)
- smaller ions (higher charge density)

Down the group lower melting point:
- more shells,
- greater distance

Characteristics of metal:
- Electrical conductors (free moving electrons)
- Thermal conductors
- High melting point
- Malleable (bendable) & ductile (can be drawn into wire)
- Dense, shiny
- Soft – only alloys are hard *(white gold)*

Giant metallic lattice

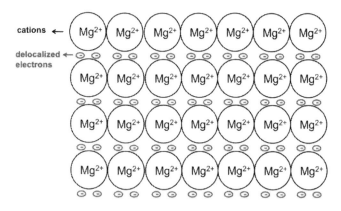

40

Giant & Simple Covalent Structures

Giant Covalent Structures

- Network of covalently bonded atoms (Macromolecula structures)
- C, Si => four covalent bonds (Group 4)

Allotropes: pure forms of the same element that differ in structure

Allotropes of carbon:
Diamond: 4 bonds, tetrahedral —> hard, cold, high melting point, not conducting electricity, not soluble
Graphite: 3 bonds, trigonal planar -> sheets of hexagons – slippery, lone electrons -> conduct electricity, strong/lightweight, insoluble

Silica (SiO_2): tetrahedral, hard, crystals, high melting point, insoluble, not conducting electricity, *hygroscopic*. (quartz, sand)

Simple covalent structures (Molecules)

Sulfur: yellow solid, simple molecules like S_8 rings *or amorphous (non-crystalline)*

Phosphorus: white solid, simple molecules like P_4

1.4 Periodicity

Periodic Table & Elements existing as diatomic molecules

Periodic Table

-> arranged by proton number

Group number
-> number of outer electrons => determines chemical properties & reactions

Period number
-> number of shells

Group Names:

Gr 1	Alkali metals
Gr 2	Alkaline earth metals
Gr 7	Halogens
Gr 8	Noble Gases
Gr III – XII	Transition metals

Mendeleev:
- Early version of periodic table
- Arranged by atomic mass
- Left gaps so elements with similar chemical properties could be in the same group

Elements existing as diatomic molecules

H_2

N_2

O_2

Halogens: F_2, Cl_2, Br_2, I_2

Have No Fear Of Ice-Cold Beer

Periodic Trends

Periodic Trends

s-block: Group 1,2
p-block: Group 3 - 8
d-block: Transition elements

Atomic radius decreases across period:
- More protons (nuclear charge) -> electrons pulled closer
- Same shell -> no extra shielding

Electronegativity increases across period
-> see revision card 'Electronegativity'

Ionisation energy increases across period
-> see revision card 'Ionisation energy'

Melting and Boiling points:
- Increase for metals across period -> see revision card "metallic bond'
- Still increase for group 4 elements -> see revision card 'giant covalent structures'
- Then increase or decrease for non-metals depending on how many atoms form simple covalent structure (van der Waals forces) -> see revision cards 'simple covalent structures' & 'Elements existing as diatomic molecules'
- Noble gases have lowest melting points due to existing as single atoms

Ionisation energy

Ionisation energy

Definition: energy required to remove one electron from **one mole** of atoms of an element in the **gaseous state** [kJ/mol]

Increases across period:
- more protons,
- same shell (smaller radius)
 => stronger nuclear attraction

Decreases down group:
- more shells, more distance
- more shielding,
- despite more protons

Reactivity
- decreases down Halogen group
- increases down Alkali group

1st Ionisation energy: $\quad O_{(g)} \rightarrow O^+_{(g)} + e^-$

2nd Ionisation energy: $\quad O^+_{(g)} \rightarrow O^{2+}_{(g)} + e^-$

2nd Ionisation energy > 1st Ionisation energy
- increasingly positive ion
- smaller ions
- less repulsion amongst remaining electrons

Big jump when new shell is broken into => closer to the nucleus

Drop in ionisation energy between Groups 2 and 3 (B)
-> start of p-subshell, which is further away from nucleus
-> full $2s^2$ subshell gives some partial shielding
-> despite increased nuclear charge

Drop between Groups 5 and 6 (O, S)
-> one orbital of the 3 p-orbitals is filled with two electrons, which repel each other

1.5 Introduction to Organic Chemistry

Naming Rules (Nomenclature)

Naming Rules (Nomenclature)

- Longest chain –> stem or prefix (Longest chain with most side-chains)

- Numbering carbons: – lowest number for functional group/side chain

- Never put side-chain on first and last carbon (not isomer, just longer chain)

- Alphabetical order for alkyl side chains (disregard di, tri) –> prefix with carbon number (3-ethyl-2,4-dimethylpentane)

- Multiple side-chains/functional groups: di, tri, tetra, (2, 3 ,4)

- Main functional group: – suffix (pentan-2-ol)

- Side chains (branched chain) alkyl groups: Methyl, Ethyl, Propyl, Butyl,…

Example:

3-ethyl-2,4-dimethylpentan-2-ol

Types of organic formulae

Types of organic formulae

2-methylpentan-1-ol:

molecular formula: $C_6H_{14}O$

structural formula: $CH_3CH_2CH_2CH(CH_3)CH_2OH$

displayed formula/structural formula (all bonds must be drawn):

skeletal formula:

General formula for all alcohols: $C_nH_{2n+1}OH$

Functional groups

Functional groups

-> groups of atoms in a molecule that are responsible for the reaction

R (residue): alkyl-group C_nH_{2n+1} : -CH_3 (methyl), -C_2H_5 (ethyl), -C_3H_7 (propyl) etc.

Alcohol   R-OH

Aldehyde:

$$R-C\overset{\displaystyle O}{\underset{H}{\diagup}}$$

Ketone:

$$R^1-C\overset{\displaystyle O}{\underset{R^2}{\diagup}}$$

Carboxylic Acid

$$R-C\overset{\displaystyle O}{\underset{OH}{\diagup}}$$

Ester:

$$R^1-C\overset{\displaystyle O}{\underset{O-R^2}{\diagup}}$$

Ether: $R^1\text{-}O\text{-}R^2$

Amine: R-NH_2

Amide (Peptide):

$$R^1-C\overset{\displaystyle O}{\underset{NH-R^2}{\diagup}}$$

Nitro: R-NO_2

Nitrile: R-CN

Three main types of organic reactions

Three main types of organic reactions

Substitution   *(e. g. nucleophilic substitution of haloalkane with OH⁻)*

Elimination   *(e.g. dehydration of alcohol)*

Addition   *(e. g. HX on double bond of alkenes)*

(Oxidation/Reduction -> inorganic)
(acid base reaction / salt formation -> inorganic)

Three main organic reaction mechanisms

nucleophilic   (likes positive charges)

electrophilic   (likes electrons/negative charges)

radical   (unpaired electron, very aggressive)

Electrophiles & Nucleophiles

Electrophiles:
-> **electron pair acceptors**

- Cations: H^+, X^+, NO_2^+, Diazonium $R-N_2^+$
- or polarized molecules like halogens X_2 (Br_2)

Nucleophiles:
-> **electron pair donor**

possess at least one lone pair of electrons (ideally anions):
- OH^-, CN^-, X^-, NH_3, H_2O, R-OH

Types of Isomers

Types of Isomers

I) Structural Isomers
Def.: same molecular formula but different structural formula

1) **Chain-Isomers**
–> chain arranged differently

$$H_3C\!-\!CH_2\!-\!CH_2\!-\!CH_3$$

butane

$$H_3C\!-\!\underset{\underset{CH_3}{|}}{CH}\!-\!CH_3$$

2-methylpropane

2) **Positional Isomers**
–> functional group at different positions

$$H_3C\!-\!CH_2\!-\!\underset{\overset{|}{OH}}{CH_2}$$

propan-1-ol

$$H_3C\!-\!\underset{\overset{|}{OH}}{HC}\!-\!CH_3$$

propan-2-ol

3) **Functional Group Isomers**
–> different functional groups

$$H_3C\!-\!CH_2\!-\!C\!\!\nearrow^{O}_{\searrow H}$$

propanal

$$H_3C\!-\!\overset{\overset{O}{\|}}{C}\!-\!CH_3$$

propanone

other examples: alcohol/ether, carboxylic acid/ester

II) Stereoisomers
Definition: same structural formula but atoms arranged differently in space

1) **E/Z isomers (Cis/Trans)**
2) **Optical Isomers**

-> see revision card 'Stereoisomers'

1.6 Alkanes

Alkanes

Alkanes

Saturated hydrocarbons (only single C-C bonds, only hydrogen and carbon)

Homologues series of alkanes: $C_n H_{2n+2}$

Methane, Ethane, Propane, Butane	-> gases
Pentane, Hexane, Heptane, Octane, Nonane, Decane	-> liquids
from C_{18}	*-> solid*

- unreactive
- only other organic reactions: **radical substitution**/elimination
- branched isomers have lower boiling point than unbranched
  - less surface area of contact
  - weaker Van der Waals forces
  - less energy required to overcome Van der Waals forces

Application:
fuel –> burning/combustion with O_2: $CO_2 + H_2O$
Limited supply of O_2 => incomplete combustion: CO - toxic
Fuel contains sulphur => SO_2 (pollution, acid rain), removed with CaO (neutralization) -> see revision card 'acid and bases – preparation' Unit 3

Preparation
from crude oil

Terms

Homologues series: Group of compound with same general formula and same functional group. They differ by a 'CH$_2$' group

Aliphatic: a compound containing carbon and hydrogen joined together in straight chains, branched chains or non-aromatic rings

Alicyclic: an aliphatic compound arranged in non-aromatic rings with or without side chains

Crude Oil – Fuel

Crude oil - fuel

- crude oil consists of hydrocarbons with different chain length.
- In a petroleum refinery, these are separated, in different fractions, according to their boiling point by fractional distillation (heating then cooling in tower -> condensation)
- the longer the chain the higher the boiling point (bottom of fractionating/cooling tower)

different fractions:

<RT	Gases	$C_1 - C_4$
	LPG, camping gas	
< 40 C	Petrol (gasoline)	$C_5 - C_{12}$
	petrol	
<110 C	Naphtha	$C_7 - C_{14}$
	petrochemicals	
<180 C	Kerosene (paraffin)	$C_{11} - C_{15}$
	jet fuel, central heating, petrochemicals	
<250 C	Gas-Oil (diesel)	$C_{15} - C_{19}$
	diesel, central heating	
<340 C	Mineral-Oil	$C_{20} - C_{30}$
	lubricating oil	
>350 C	Residue: Fuel-Oil	$C_{30} - C_{40}$
	ships, power stations	
	Wax, grease	$C_{40} - C_{50}$
	candles, lubrication	
	Bitumen	C_{50+}
	road, roofing	

Cracking

long chains are broken down by Cracking to produce more small and middle chains,
-> More demand for petrol ($C_4 - C_{10}$), naphtha ($C_7 - C_{14}$ – petrochemicals) & alkenes

Thermal Cracking

thermal decomposition through heating (800 – 1000 C)
Naphtha -> alkenes (for plastics) & side products (alkanes – straight/branched/cyclic)

Catalytic Cracking

Thermal decomposition (450 C) with steam and catalyst Al_2O_3 (zeolite) under slight pressure
Bitumen -> fuel & arenes

Greenhouse effect

Greenhouse effect

Greenhouse gases:
- H_2O, CO_2, CH_4
- absorb IR radiation -> bonds vibrate

Mechanism:
- *Earth absorbs UV/Vis light and heats up*
- *heat is normally radiated back into space through IR window (IR frequencies not absorbed by atmospheric gases)*
- *greenhouse gases in troposphere absorb other IR frequencies and remit back to earth causing global warming (rise of sea levels, climate change).*

Contribution depends on
- *How much Radiation absorbed by molecules*
- *Concentration of gas*

Scientific evidence for global warming:
- *Average temperature increased*
- *CO_2 levels increased*
- *Sea water more acidic (H_2CO_3)*

Unit 2 – Chemistry in Action

2.1 Energetics

Enthalpy Changes - Definitions

Enthalpy Changes - Definitions

Exothermic $-\Delta H_r$ negative: energy released into surroundings
                     -> heats up

Endothermic $+\Delta H_r$ positive: energy taken from surroundings
                     -> cools down

ΔH_r : enthalpy change of the reaction **[KJ mol^{-1}]**

Enthalpy change: Heat/energy change in a reaction at constant pressure

Standard enthalpy change $^{\ominus}$: under standard conditions: 1 atm/100 kPa, 298 K

~ **of reactions, $\Delta H_r^{\ominus}$**: is the enthalpy change when the reaction occurs in the **molar quantities** shown in the **chemical equation**, under **standard conditions** in their **standard states**.

~ **of formation $\Delta H_f^{\ominus}$** of a compound: is the enthalpy change when **1 mole** of a **compound** is formed from its **elements** in their **standard states** under **standard conditions**: 298 K, 1 atm.
$2C_{(s)} + 3H_{2(g)} + \frac{1}{2} O_2(g) \rightarrow C_2H_5OH$

~ **of combustion $\Delta H_c^{\ominus}$**: is the enthalpy change when **1 mole** of a substance is **completely burned in oxygen** under **standard conditions**

~ **of atomization $\Delta H_{at}^{\ominus}$**: is the enthalpy change when **1 mole** of **gaseous atoms** is formed from the element in its **standard state**
$\frac{1}{2} Cl_{2(g)} \rightarrow Cl_{(g)}$

~ **of neutralization $\Delta H_{neut}^{\ominus}$**: is the enthalpy change when **1 mole of water** is formed from the neutralization of **(H$^+$) hydrogen ions** by (OH$^-$) **hydroxide ions** under **standard conditions**
$H^+_{(aq)} + OH^-_{(aq)} \rightarrow H_2O_{(l)}$

Calorimeter

Calorimeter

q = mcΔT

q: enthalpy change [Joules]
m: mass of water [g]
c: specific heat capacity of water (4.18 J g^{-1} K^{-1} -> data sheet)
ΔT: temperature change [C]

Reasons why enthalpy change is underestimated by experiment
- Heat absorbed by container
- Heat lost to surroundings
- Incomplete combustion
- Evaporation of volatile fuel
- Non-standard conditions

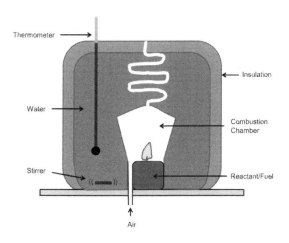

Calorimeter

Hess's law

Hess's law:

The total enthalpy change for a reaction is independent of the route taken (as long as the initial and final conditions are the same)

-> To calculate enthalpy changes for unknown reactions from known reactions (e.g. reaction enthalpies from formation enthalpies)

$$\Delta H_r = \Sigma \Delta H_f \text{ (products)} - \Sigma \Delta H_f \text{ (reactants)}$$

ΔH_r : Enthalpy change of reaction [kJ mol^{-1}]
ΔH_f : Enthalpy change of formation [kJ mol^{-1}]
$\Delta H_r^{\ominus}$: Enthalpy change of reaction with elements in their standard states under standard conditions (1 atm/100 kPa, 298 K)

-> Elements like O_2 have no formation enthalpy (zero)

Triangles/arrows
Add arrows going to the same products (endpoint) of the unknown enthalpy using the alternative route:
going along arrow -> positive sign, against arrow -> negative sign for enthalpy

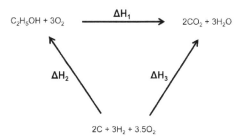

$$\Delta H_1 = -\Delta H_2 + \Delta H_3$$

Example Calculation for standard enthalpy change of combustion for ethanol:

$\Delta H_f^{\ominus} (CO_2) =$	-394 kJ mol^{-1}
$\Delta H_f^{\ominus} (H_2O) =$	-286 kJ mol^{-1}
$\Delta H_f^{\ominus} (C_2H_5OH) =$	-277 kJ mol^{-1}
$\Delta H_f^{\ominus} (C, O_2, H_2) =$	0 kJ mol^{-1}

$\Delta H_r \quad = \Sigma \Delta H_f \text{ (products)} \quad - \quad \Sigma \Delta H_f \text{ (reactants)}$

$\Delta H_c \quad = [(2x{-}394) + (3x{-}286)] \quad - \quad [-277] \qquad | \text{ kJ mol}^{-1}$

$\qquad = \textbf{-1369} \text{ kJ mol}^{-1}$

Bond enthalpies

Bond enthalpies

ΔH_r: enthalpy change of reaction:

$$\Delta H_r = \Sigma H \text{ bonds broken} - \Sigma H \text{ bonds formed}$$
or
$$\Delta H_r = \Sigma H \text{ bonds (reactants)} - \Sigma H \text{ bonds (products)}$$

Bond dissociation enthalpy: average bond dissociation enthalpy per mole of gaseous compound [kJ mol^{-1}]

Mean bond enthalpy: average enthalpy required to dissociate a covalent bond over different compounds.

-> **always positive** (also for bonds formed)

If ΣH bonds formed > ΣH bonds broken => exothermic

If ΣH bonds formed < ΣH bonds broken => endothermic

2.2 Kinetics

Rates of reactions

Rates of reactions

Rates (speed) depend on:
- temperature
- surface area (size of particles)
- catalyst
- concentration of reactants *(solvent)*
- pressure for gases

Rate of reaction: change of concentration (product or reactant) over time

$$r = \frac{\Delta c}{\Delta t}$$

Graph: shows increase/decrease over time

Measurement:
- Precipitation (marker disappears)
- Change in mass when gas given off (balance)
- Volume of gas given off (syringe)

Collision Theory:
- Higher Temperature -> higher speed => more successful collisions ($E_{kin} > E_a$)
- Higher concentration -> collision more likely
- Larger surface area -> particles can access more area
- Catalyst -> see revision card 'catalyst'

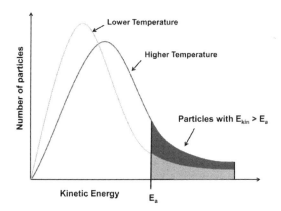

Temperature Increase

-> graphs should not touch y-axis

75

Catalyst

<u>Catalyst</u>

Speeds up chemical reactions (increases rate) by **lowering activation energy** (more successful collisions) and providing an **alternative reaction pathway**.
Catalysts are **not used up** during the reactions **(unchanged).**

- **Mechanism:**
    - **adsorption** of reactant at catalyst surface
    - this **weakens bonds** in reactant (lowers activation energy)
    - **new bonds** of product are formed
    - **desorption** of products after reaction.
- **homogenous catalyst** => same physical state:
  enzymes/substrate (l/l) or H_2SO_4 (l/l)
- **heterogeneous catalyst** => different physical states: catalytic
  converter Pt/Rh (s/g):
  $2CO + 2NO -> 2CO_2 + N_2$
  other examples: Ni, Fe, V_2O_5
  contact process: $V_2O_5 + SO_2 -> V_2O_4 + SO_3$,
  $V_2O_4 + \frac{1}{2}O_2 -> V_2O_5$
- **does not change chemical equilibrium**
- **Catalyst poison**: binds stronger to catalyst than reactant ->
  blocking surface

Mechanism:

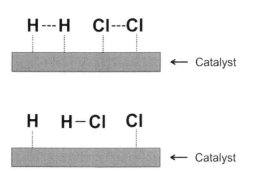

Enthalpy profile diagram of exothermic reaction with and without catalyst

Enthalpy profile diagram of exothermic reaction with and without catalyst

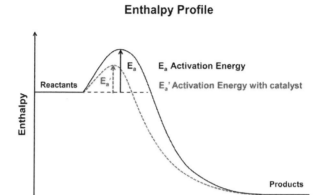

Enthalpy Profile

Maxwell-Boltzmann Distribution

Maxwell-Boltzmann Distribution

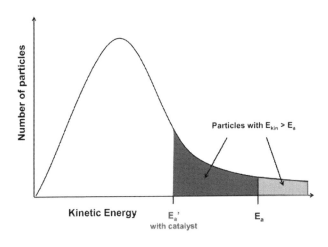

2.3 Equilibria

Equilibrium and Reversible Reactions

Equilibrium and Reversible Reactions

Reversible reaction: products convert back to reactants (reaction goes both ways)
 => incomplete reaction

Dynamic equilibrium (steady state)
-> rates of the forward and reverse reactions are equal
- both reactions still going on, balance => low percentage of product
- **concentrations** of reactants and products remain **constant**
- only in **closed system**

-> Important for yield in chemical industry:

Le Chetallier: when the conditions of a system at equilibrium changes, the position of the equilibrium shifts in the direction that opposes (counteracts) the change

Ammonia manufacture (Haber-process): iron catalyst (*200 atm, 450 C)*

N_2 (g) + $3H_2$ (g) $\leftrightarrows$ $2NH_3$ (g) $\Delta H - 93$ kJ/mol (exothermic)

+ pressure	-> shifts to the side with less moles gas (here to the right)
+ heat	-> shifts in the direction of endothermic process (here to the left)
+ concentration reactants	-> shifts to right
- concentration products	-> shifts to right

=> Catalyst does not change equilibrium but increases rate of both reactions (equilibrium is reached faster)

For **Methanol production** see revision card 'Alcohols' 2.10

2.4 Redox Reactions

Redox reactions – Oxidation states

Redox reactions – Oxidation states

Oxidation **I**s **L**oss of electrons
-> oxidation state becomes more positive

Reduction **I**s **G**ain of electrons
-> oxidation state becomes more negative

=> OILRIG

Oxidation states/numbers
-> help to determine chemical formula of compound

Def: identical to the charge of ions in a salt;
the charge an element would have, in a molecule, if it were a salt.

Rules:
- always zero for pure element in its basic state (free, uncombined element)
- group number indicates maximum oxidation state
- most common oxidation states in compounds:
  Halogens   -1
  Oxygen   -2 (-1)
  Hydrogen   +1 (-1)
  Metals positive (alkali metals +1, alkaline earth metals +2)

Oxidising agent: gets reduced (helps other element to get oxidised)

Reducing agent: gets oxidised (helps other element to get reduced)

Disproportionation

Def: same element gets reduced and oxidized

-> Special kind of Redox reaction

$$Cu_2O + 2H^+ \;\text{->}\; Cu^{2+} + Cu + H_2O$$
$${\scriptstyle +1}\phantom{+ 2H^+ \;\text{->}\;} {\scriptstyle +2} {\scriptstyle 0}$$

-> see also revision card 'Water treatment'

Balancing Redox Equations

Balancing Redox Equations

How to balance a simple redox equation

- First write the chemical formula of the product to the right side of the arrow. Balance this formula with lower case numbers according to oxidation states (group number) by using lowest common multiple.
- Then balance equation by putting numbers in front of partners (never change lower case numbers, as this would create a different substance)

$$4Al + 3O_2 \rightarrow 2Al_2O_3$$

$\quad 0 \quad\quad 0 \quad\quad\quad +3 \;\; -2 \quad$ **(lowest common multiple: 6)**

If not just elements reacting (ions/molecules):

- First balance electrons, starting with the biggest difference in oxidation states (between left and right side of equation)
- then balance all the other partners (oxygen before hydrogen)

$$8I^- + 8H^+ + H_2SO_4 \rightarrow 4I_2 + H_2S + 4H_2O$$

$\quad -1 \quad\quad\quad +6 \quad\quad\quad 0 \quad -2$

Biggest difference: **S: +6 -> -2** $\quad\quad$ => gains **8e⁻**

I⁻: -1 -> 0 => loses 1e⁻ => **8I⁻** needed

- **number of electrons lost and gained must be the same!**
- charges have to be balanced as well ($8I^- = 8H^+$)

For half-equations see revision card 'electrode potentials' A2

Two main types of inorganic reactions

Two main types of inorganic reactions

1) Redox (Reduction/Oxidation)

-> transfer of electrons (Oxidation states change)

$$\underset{0}{4Al} + \underset{0}{3O_2} \; -> \; \underset{+3 \; -2}{2Al_2O_3}$$

-> **Displacement** & **Disproportionation** are special cases of Redox reactions

2) Acid-Base

-> transfer of protons H^+ (Oxidation states do not change)

$$\underset{+1 \; -1}{HCl} + \underset{+1 \; -2 \; +1}{NaOH} \; -> \; \underset{+1 \; -1}{NaCl} + \underset{+1 \; -2}{H_2O}$$

Minor reaction types

- Thermal decomposition
  $$CaCO_{3(s)} \; -> \; CaO(s) + CO_{2(g)}$$

- Precipitation
  $$Ag^+_{(aq)} + Cl^-_{(aq)} \; -> \; AgCl_{(s)}$$

-> No change of oxidation states

2.5 Group 7 The Halogens

Group 7 Halogens

Group 7 Halogens

-> Diatomic molecules (see revision card 'Diatomic molecules' 3.1)

F_2	yellow gas	very toxic	
Cl_2	green gas	toxic	bleaches litmus paper
Br_2	red-brown liquid	toxic	
I_2	black-purple solid		

Strong oxidizing agents
Metal + Halogen -> Halide salts (redox)
$2Na$ + Cl_2 -> $2NaCl$

Less electronegative down group
-> see revision card 'Electronegativity'

Less reactive down group
-> see revision card 'Ionization energy'

Melting/boiling points increase down group
- larger molecules
- more electrons
-> stronger Van der Waals

Reactions of Chlorine with water and NaOH
-> see revision card 'water treatment'

Water treatment

Water treatment

Water treatment (drinking water/swimming pool)

$$\underset{0}{Cl_2} + H_2O \ -> \ \underset{+1}{HClO} \ + \ \underset{-1}{HCl} -> \textbf{Disproportionation (see rev. card)}$$

HClO chloric(I) acid (hypochlorous acid) -> dissociates into H^+ and ClO^- ions

ClO^- chlorate(I) ion: strong oxidising agent -> kills bacteria & algae

Disadvantages:

- Cl_2 harmful and toxic $->$ irritates respiratory system; liquid chlorine burns skin/eyes
- Cl_2 reacts with organic compounds to form chlorinated hydrocarbons $->$ carcinogenic

Bleach Preparation

$$Cl_2 + 2NaOH -> \textbf{NaClO} + NaCl + H_2O$$

Condition: cold, dilute sodiumhydroxide

Bleach: NaClO Sodium hypochlorite, chlorate (I) - strong oxidising agent (disinfectant)

Iodine tablets (camping – drinking water)

$$I_2 + H_2O -> HI + HIO$$

F^- **ions** prevent tooth decay

Hot concentrated NaOH solution:

$$\underset{0}{3Cl_2} + 6NaOH -> \underset{+5}{NaClO_3} + \underset{-1}{5NaCl} + 3H_2O$$

$$Chlorate(V)$$

$$\underset{0}{3Br_2} + \underset{-2\ +1}{6OH^-} -> \underset{+5\ -2}{BrO_3^-} + \underset{-1}{5Br^-} + \underset{+1\ -2}{3H_2O}$$

$$Bromate(V)$$

Reaction of chlorine with water in sunlight:

$$2Cl_2 + 2H_2O \ -> \ 4HCl + O_2$$

Halides

Halides

Test for Halide Ions

-> with acidified (HNO_3) **$AgNO_3$** solution:

Halide	Precipitate	Dissolves in
F^-	-	
Cl^-	white	diluted NH_3
Br^-	cream	conc NH_3
I^-	yellow	insoluble

Displacement reactions
-> other Test for Halides -> See revision card 'Displacement'

Reducing agent
-> power increases down group (more shells, more shielding)

Reactions of Halide ions with H_2SO_4

NaF or NaCl with H_2SO_4:
$NaF_{(s)} + H_2SO_{4(aq)} \rightarrow NaHSO_{4(s)} + HF_{(g)}$ -> acid/base
$NaCl_{(s)} + H_2SO_{4(aq)} \rightarrow NaHSO_{4(s)} + HCl_{(g)}$ -> **test for HCl see below**

NaBr with H_2SO_4
$NaBr_{(s)} + H_2SO_{4(aq)} \rightarrow NaHSO_{4(s)} + HBr_{(g)}$
$2HBr_{(aq)} + H_2SO_{4(aq)} \rightarrow SO_{2(g)} + H_2O_{(l)} + Br_{2(g)}$ -> **Brown Fumes (redox)**
    -1   +6   +4   0

NaI with H_2SO_4
$NaI_{(s)} + H_2SO_{4(aq)} \rightarrow NaHSO_{4(s)} + HI_{(g)}$
$2HI_{(g)} + H_2SO_{4(aq)} \rightarrow SO_{2(g)} + H_2O_{(l)} + I_{2(g)}$ -> **Purple vapour (redox)**
   -1   +6   +4   0

$6HI_{(g)} + SO_{2(g)} \rightarrow H_2S_{(g)} + 3I_{2(s)} + H_2O_{(l)}$ -> **H_2S toxic, smelly gas**
   -1   +4   -2   0

Hydrogen Halides
- Colourless acidic gases
- turn blue litmus paper red
- Test for HCl:
  $NH_{3(g)} + HCl_{(g)} \rightarrow NH_4Cl_{(s)}$ -> white fumes

Test for ions & Displacement Reaction

Test for ions

Carbonates: $CO_3^{2-} + 2H^+ \rightarrow H_2O + CO_2$ fizzing

Sulphate: $Ba^{2+}_{(aq)} + SO_4^{2-}_{(aq)} \rightarrow BaSO_{4(s)}$ **white precipitate**

Ammonium: $NH_4^+ + OH^- \rightarrow H_2O + NH_3$ litmus: red -> blue

Halides: $Ag^+_{(aq)} + X^-_{(aq)} \rightarrow AgX_{(s)}$ **precipitate**

X^-: halide ion (Cl^-, Br^-, I^-)
-> see revision card 'Group 7 Halides'

Displacement Reaction

- to identify halide ions
- more reactive halogen displaces (oxidises) less reactive
-> above in group, higher oxidizing strength
- special type of Redox reaction
- shake solution with hexane/cyclohexane (non-polar solvent, better for dissolving halogen)

$$Cl_2 + 2Br^- \rightarrow Br_2 + 2Cl^-$$
$$0 \quad-1 \quad0 \quad-1$$

	Water	Hexane
F_2 yellow gas	-	-
Cl_2 green gas	colourless	pale green
Br_2 red-brown liquid	yellow/orange	orange/red
I_2 black-purple solid	brown	pink/violet

Solubility

Solubility

How soluble a salt is depends on its characteristics *(K_{sp}-solubility product constant)* and cannot usually be predicted from its chemical formula, but can be experimentally determined.

Common insoluble salts:
- silver halides
- barium sulfate
- most carbonates - except sodium, potassium, ammonium carbonates

Common soluble salts:
- most hydrogen carbonates like $NaHCO_3$ (baking soda)
- most sodium salts

Solvents:
- salts and polar molecules are soluble in polar solvents like water
- non polar molecules like halogens or hydrocarbons are soluble in non-polar solvents like cyclohexane

List of Anions & Naming Salts

List of Anions

chloride	Cl^-
carbonate	CO_3^{2-}
hydroxide	OH^-
sulphate	SO_4^{2-}
sulphite/sulphate(IV)	SO_3^{2-}
sulphide	S^{2-}
nitrate	NO_3^-
nitrite/nitrate(IV)	NO_2^-
phosphate	PO_4^{3-}
ethanoate/acetate	CH_3COO^-
cyanide	CN^-

Naming salts

First cation (metal, +) then anion (non-metal, -): e.g. NaCl -> sodium chloride

Name of **anion (negative ion)** finishes with:

- ide -> if anion consists of just one element like S^{2-}, e. g. Ca**S** – calcium sulph**ide** or NaCl – sodium chlor**ide**

- ate -> anion consists of more than one elements like SO_4^{2-} (oxygen & sulphur) and sulphur is in its highest oxidation state (+6): e. g. Na$_2$**SO$_4$** – Sodium sulph**ate** -> **or sulphate(VI)**

- ite -> anion with more than one element (oxygen & sulphur) and sulphur is in its second highest oxidation state (+4) for example Na$_2$SO$_3$ – Sodium sul**fite** -> **or sulphate(IV)**
-> **can also be named sulphate(IV): write oxidation state as roman numeral in brackets**
=> **use this as general method for naming anions with more than one element**

2.6 Group 2 The Alkaline Earth Metals

Group 2 – Alkaline Earth Metals

Group 2 – Alkaline Earth Metals

Reactions of the Alkaline Earth Metals

React with water to produce hydroxides and hydrogen gas
$Mg_{(s)} + 2H_2O_{(l)} \rightarrow Mg(OH)_{2(aq)} + H_{2(g)}$

They burn in oxygen with characteristic colour
$2Ca_{(s)} + O_{2(g)} \rightarrow 2CaO_{(s)}$ (brick red)
Mg -> brilliant white flame

Group 2 oxides, hydroxides are bases
- $Mg(OH)_2$ Neutralises stomach acid (indigestion tablets)
- $Ca(OH)_2$ Neutralises acid soils (agriculture)
-> see revision card 'bases' Unit 3

Solubility trends of Group 2 metals
Singly charged anions (OH^-)   -> increased solubility down group
double charged anions (SO_4^{2-}) -> decreased solubility down group

Hydroxides	more soluble
Sulphates	less soluble
Carbonates	less soluble

Test for sulfate or Ba^{2+} ions: add $BaCl_2$ solution
$Ba^{2+}_{(aq)} + SO_4^{2-}{}_{(aq)} \rightarrow BaSO_{4(s)}$ (white precipitate)

Barium meals
- Barium sulfate absorbs X-rays.
- Used in medicine to show soft tissue in X-rays.

Periodic Trends of Alkaline Earth Metals

Atomic & Ionic Radius increases down group
-> more shells

Ionisation Energy decreases down group
=> Reactivity increases down group
-> see revision card 'Ionisation energy'

Melting Points decrease down group
-> see revision card 'Metallic bonding'

2.7 Extraction of Metals

Extracting Metals from Ores

Extracting Metals from Ores

Ores: metal oxides or sulfides
-> Reduce to get pure metal (element)
-> use carbon/coke or CO as reducing agent (cheap)

Iron
Blast furnace (smelting):
Reduction of Hematite Fe_2O_3, Pyrite FeS_2
$Fe_2O_3 + 3CO -> 2Fe + 3CO_2$
$2Fe_2O_3 + 3C -> 4Fe + 3CO_2$

If sulfide -> first oxidation (roasting):
$2ZnS + 3O_2 -> 2ZnO + 2SO_2$
SO_2 pollutants; but can be used for contact process (H_2SO_4)

Manganese
Reduction of Manganese (IV) oxide
$MnO_2 + C -> Mn + CO_2$
$MnO_2 + 2CO -> Mn + 2CO_2$

Copper
Reduction of Coppercarbonate (malachite)
$2CuCO_3 + C -> 2Cu + 3CO_2$
$CuCO_3 -> CuO + CO_2$
$2CuO + C -> 2Cu + CO_2$

Aluminium: too reactive to get reduced by C, melting point too high 2050 C
Electrolysis:
Al_2O_3 (bauxite) molten with **Na_3AlF_6 (cryolite)** which lowers melting point
to 970 C
Cathode (carbon lining):   **$Al^{3+} + 3e^- -> Al$**
Anode (carbon/graphite):   **$2O^{2-} -> O_2 + 4e^-$**
-> High usage of electricity makes it **expensive** (hydroelectric power station)

Tungsten
Reduced with C -> too brittle
Pure tungsten is reduced by hydrogen H_2 (expensive, explosive!):
$WO_{3(s)} + 3H_{2(g)} -> W_{(s)} + 3H_2O_{(g)}$ (furnace, 700 C)

Titanium (TiO_2) reduction with Na or Mg in several steps
1) $TiO_{2(s)} + 2Cl_{2(g)} + 2C_{(s)} -> TiCl_{4(s)} + 2CO_{(g)}$ (900 C)
2) Fractional distillation of $TiCl_{4(s)}$ under Ar or N_2
3) $TiCl_{4(s)} + 4Na_{(l)} -> Ti_{(s)} + 4NaCl_{(l)}$ (furnace, 1000 C)
or $TiCl_{4(s)} + 2Mg_{(l)} -> Ti_{(s)} + 2MgCl_{2(l)}$ (furnace, 1000 C)

Environmental aspects of metal extraction

Environmental aspects of metal extraction

Advantages of recycling metals
- saves raw materials
- saves energy
- reduces waste
- reduces land use

Disadvantages
- collecting and sorting expensive
- purity varies
- not consistent supply

Copper extraction with scrap iron
Ore dissolved in acidified water and iron added

$Cu^{2+}_{(aq)} + Fe_{(s)} \rightarrow Cu_{(s)} + Fe^{2+}_{(aq)}$ (reduction)
- for low grade ore (low percentage of copper)
- slower and lower yield than carbon reduction
- cheaper (lower temperature) and less CO_2 (environment)

2.8 Haloalkanes

Radical Substitution in Alkanes

Radical Substitution in Alkanes

Radical: species with unpaired electron

Homolytic fission: each atom receives one bond electron, radicals are formed

$$Cl \overset{\frown}{-} Cl \xrightarrow{\text{UV}} Cl \cdot \ + \ Cl \cdot$$

Heterolytic fission: one atom receives both bond electrons, ions are formed

$$Cl - Cl \ \to \ Cl^- \ + \ Cl^+$$

Initiation:

$$Cl - Cl \xrightarrow{\text{UV}} Cl \cdot \ + \ Cl \cdot$$

A few radicals are formed by photodisssociation (most of Cl_2 still intact)

Propagation (chain reaction)

$$H-\underset{\underset{H}{|}}{\overset{\overset{H}{|}}{C}}-H \ + \ Cl \cdot \longrightarrow CH_3 \cdot \ + \ HCl$$

$$CH_3 \cdot \ + \ Cl-Cl \longrightarrow H_3C-Cl \ + \ Cl \cdot$$

- radical substitution of H atoms with halogen atoms => haloalkanes
- chain reaction continues until all H are substituted
=> **mixture of products:** (monochloro-, dichloro-, trichloromethane and tetrachloromethane)

Curly arrows:
- full headed - **movement of a pair of electrons**
- half headed – **movement of a single electron**

Termination:

$$Cl \cdot \ + \ Cl \cdot \ \to \ Cl_2$$
$$CH_3 \cdot \ + \ CH_3 \cdot \longrightarrow H_3C-CH_3$$
$$CH_3 \cdot \ + \ Cl \cdot \longrightarrow H_3C-Cl$$

Overall reaction:

$$CH_4 \ + \ Cl_2 \ \to \ CH_3Cl \ + \ HCl$$

Ozone layer & CFCs

Ozone layer & CFCs

Radical: unpaired (single) electron (highly reactive)
=> see also revision card 'radical substitution on alkanes'

Ozone protects us (stratosphere, absorbs UVA,B,C => damage body)

Ozone layer is constantly replaced:

$$O_2 + h\nu\ (UV) \rightarrow O\cdot + O\cdot$$

$$O_2 + O\cdot \rightleftarrows O_3$$

CFCs (chlorofluorocarbons) and NO_x break down ozone layer:

Initiation:

$$CFCl_3 \rightarrow CFCl_2\cdot + Cl\cdot \qquad \textbf{(UV)}$$

Propagation:

$$R\cdot + O_3 \rightarrow RO\cdot + O_2$$

$$RO\cdot + O\cdot \rightarrow R\cdot + O_2$$

-> Radical **R·** is regenerated (R = X· or NO·) => **catalyst**

- CFCs used as **solvents** and propellants
  They are inert and very stable -> live long enough to reach stratosphere
- Montreal protocol to reduce CFCs and protect ozone layer
- **Alternatives: HCFC** (hydrochlorofluorocarbons) **& HFC & Hydrocarbons**
  less stable -> broken down before reaching ozone layer

Haloalkanes

Haloalkanes (Halogenoalkanes)

Can be made by radical substitution of alkanes -> see card 'Radical substitution on Alkanes'
Naming: 2-Bromo-1-Chloroethane (alphabetically)

Reactivity
- bigger halogen atom -> weaker C-X bond, more reactive, higher rate (I>Br>Cl>F)
- tested with hot $AgNO_3$ -> precipitation at different rates

C-X polar bond (different electronegativities) => X good **leaving group** -> likes to undergo **nucleophilic substitution**

Mechanism:

-> heterolytic fission of haloalkane (hydrolysis)

Hydrolysis of Haloalkanes: nucleophilic substitution

$R-X + OH^-$ -> $R-OH + X^-$
Conditions: Warm aqueous diluted sodium hydroxide solution

$R-X + H_2O$ -> $R-OH + HX$
Conditions: Warming

$R-X + 2NH_3$ -> $R-NH_2 + NH_4X$
Conditions: Heating, reflux, pressure, in ethanol

$R-X + KCN$ -> $R-CN + KX$
Conditions: Warm, potassium cyanide in ethanol, => nitrile => *increase of chain length*
$R-CN + 2H_2O + H^+$ -> $R-COOH + NH_4^+$ (acid hydrolysis)

Elimination -> competing with substitution,
-> favored when more heating, reflux, anhydrous (ethanol) and conc. NaOH
-> OH^- acts as base for H^+ from hydrocarbon

Hydrolysis & Condensation

Hydrolysis & Condensation

Hydrolysis:
braking of covalent bonds by reaction with water (or adding H^+/OH^-)

Condensation:
reaction in which two molecules combine to form a larger one and in which water or another small molecule (HCl, methanol, acetic acid) is formed (lost)

2.9 Alkenes

Stereoisomers

Stereoisomers

Definition: same structural formula but atoms arranged differently in space

I) E/Z isomerism (Cis/Trans – if just two different groups)

Conditions
- **Double bond** (can't rotate because of π-bond)
- at least **2 different atoms/groups attached to two different** carbon atoms

Shape: trigonal planar, 120

E (trans)   **Z (cis)**

Priority (Cahn-Ingold-Prelog)
-> the higher **atomic number** the higher priority

E (trans)   **Z (cis)**

Alkenes – Reaction with Halogens

Alkenes – Reaction with Halogens

Unsaturated hydrocarbons (C=C double bonds) -> reactive
General Formula: C_nH_{2n} -> same as cyclic Alkanes

Naming:

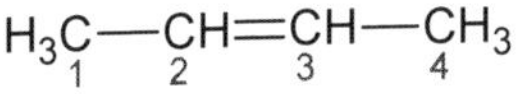

$$H_3C \underset{1}{} - \underset{2}{CH} = \underset{3}{CH} - \underset{4}{CH_3}$$

but-2-ene

double bond: **high electron density** => **electrophilic Addition**

Reactions:
I) Halogenation – electrophilic Addition

Addition of Halogens (X_2: F_2, Cl_2, Br_2, I_2)

Alkene + X_2 -> Halogenoalkane (disubstituted)

-> bromine (brown-red) gets decolourised
Conditions: spontaneous at RT (room temperature)

Mechanism:

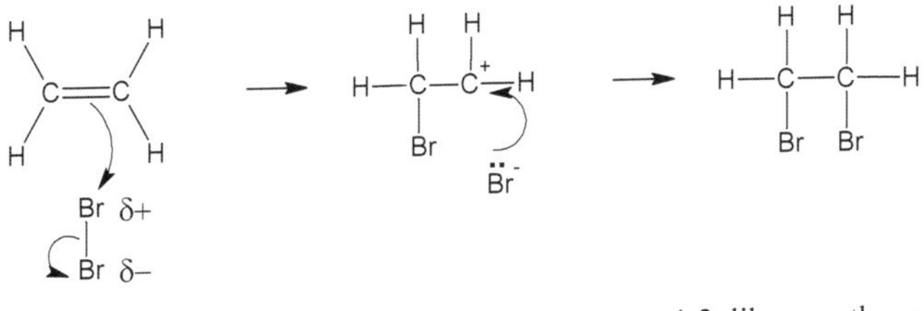

Induced dipole   Carbocation   1,2 dibromoethane
-> heterolytic fission

Test for alkenes:
bromine water: orange -> colourless
-> shake at RT

Alkenes - Addition of Hydrogen Halides

Alkenes - Addition of Hydrogen Halides

Alkene + HX -> Halogenoalkane (monosubstituted)

Mechanism:

Permanent Dipole   Secondary carbocation   2-bromopropane (major)

1-bromoepropane (minor product)

Markovnikov's rule for electrophilic Addition on **unsymmetrical alkene** with H-X (H-Br):
Halide (X^-) will go to carbon with more alkyl groups (*H^+ will go to carbon with less alkyl substituents*)

Reason: Inductive (+I) effect of alkyl groups stabilizes carbocation (primary, secondary, tertiary) by pushing electrons down

Alkenes – Hydration & Fermentation

<u>**Alkenes – Hydration & Fermentation**</u>

II) Hydration to produce alcohols

Ethene + H_2O $\rightleftharpoons$ Ethanol   (electrophilic addition)

1) Steam Hydration
Condition: acid catalyst H_3PO_4 (on silica), 300 C (exothermic), 60 – 70 atm
Equilibrium with low yield -> unreacted ethene is separated and recycled back into reactor

2) Hydration with sulfuric acid (catalyst) and warm water

Compare with fermentation

Method	Rate	Quality	Material	Process
Hydration	Very fast	Pure	Ethene (Oil)	Continuous, exp. equipment, low labour
Fermentation	Very slow	Impure	Sugars (renewable)	Batch, cheap, high labour

Conditions for fermentation:
- yeast
- anaerobic
- correct Temperature: 30 – 40 C

Fermentation reaction: $C_6H_{12}O_6$ -> $2C_2H_5OH + 2CO_2$

Applications:
- **carbon neutral fuel/petrol**
- drinks
- solvent (polar, non-polar, ionic)
- plastics
- dyes

Carbon neutral: an activity that has no net annual carbon (greenhouse gas) emissions to the atmosphere.

Polymers

Polymers

Long chain molecules of monomers *(poly – many)*

Propene
Monomer

poly(propene)
Repeating unit / Repeat unit

-> draw square bracket through middle of bond
-> polymer chain is built only from carbons with a double bond, all other carbons form side chains
-> do not forget n on both sides of equation

Alkenes:
- **addition polymerization**
- 100 % atom economy (no waste products)
- Peroxide initiators (high temperature / pressure)
- Radical mechanism

Name from monomer:
  Polyethene – cheap, strong, moulded => bags, bottles, bowls
  Polypropene – strong fibres, high elasticity => crates, robes, carpets (recycled)
  Polystyrene – cheap, moulded, foam => outer cases, packaging
  Polytetrafluoroethene (PTFE, Teflon) - inert, non-stick -> coating frying pans
  PVC (polyvinyl chloride/polychloroethene) – waterproof sheets, hard, flexible => sheets, wire insulation, records
-> Not biodegradable

Disposing:
- Landfill
- Burning: toxic gases - HCl neutralized by bases (NaOH) in scrubbers
- Recycling: sorting -> cracking or remoulding -> new plastics

2.10 Alcohols

Alcohols

Alcohols

| **Propan-1-ol** | **Propan-2-ol** | **2-Methyl-propan-2-ol** |
| Primary (1st degree) | Secondary (2) | Tertiary (3) |

-> high boiling point (hydrogen bonds)

C-O bond **polar** (different electronegativities) => **OH** good **leaving group**
-> elimination and nucleophilic substitution reactions

Dehydration of alcohol -> Elimination reaction (Condensation)

    alcohol   ->   alkene   +   water

Conditions: heating under reflux with H_2SO_{4conc} or H_3PO_4 as catalyst

Nucleophilic substitution with halide ions

Alcohol + HX -> Haloalkane + H_2O

Oxidation of Alcohols

-> with acidified (H_2SO_4) potassium dichromate $K_2Cr_2O_7$ ($^{+6}$) -> Cr^{3+}

    orange -> green

[O]: oxidising unit (2e$^-$ gained)

$$\text{Primary alcohol} + [O] \xrightarrow{\text{distillation, limited}} \textbf{aldehyde} + H_2O \;\; + [O] \xrightarrow{\text{reflux, excess}} \textbf{carboxylic acid}$$

$$\text{Primary alcohol} + 2[O] \xrightarrow{\text{reflux, excess}} \textbf{carboxylic acid} + H_2O$$

$$\text{Secondary alcohol} + [O] \xrightarrow{\text{reflux}} \textbf{ketone} + H_2O$$

Tertiary alcohol -> does not get oxidised

Burning/Combustion

$C_2H_5OH + 3O_2 \rightarrow 2CO_2 + 3H_2O$

Methanol production:

$2H_2 + CO \rightleftharpoons CH_3OH$ $\Delta H = -90 \text{ kJ mol-1}$

Conditions: 250 C, 50 – 100 atm, $Cu/ZnO/Al_2O_3$-catalyst
-> carbon neutral fuel, white spirit

Naming Aldehydes & Ketones

Aldehydes/Ketones

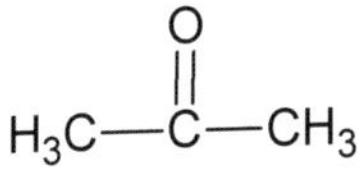

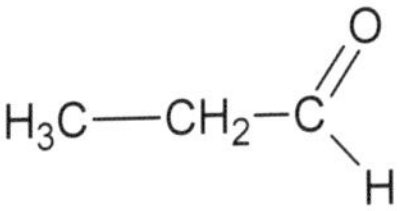

Propanone (propan-2-one)

Propanal

CH₃COCH₃

CH₃CH₂CHO

do not write: CH₃CH₂COH

2.11 Analytical Techniques

Mass Spectrometry

Mass Spectrometry

Applications: Relative Atomic/Molecular mass, Identifying organic molecules, control of synthesis, radiocarbon dating (archaeology)

Steps in a Mass spectrometer:
- Vaporisation
- Ionization
- Acceleration
- Deflection *(TOF: no deflection, time of flight proportional to mass)*
- Detection: ions cause electrical current (electrons flow from detector to +-ion) -> intensity of peak (strength of electrical current) depends on amount of ions (abundance)

=> Only positive ions are detected (always add +-sign to species)

Graph: Relative abundance % (Intensity) versus mass-to-charge ratio (m/z)

Isotope peaks: molecular M+1 peak = C^{13} -> from percentage can calculate number of carbons in molecule: C^{13} 1.1 % one C atom, 2.2 % two C etc.

Molecular ion M (peak with largest mass) => Mass of whole molecule (+1 charge)

Fragmentation (Mass Spectrum)

Example: Butan-2-one

=> $CH_3^+ = 15$ | $CO^+ = 28$ | $CH_3CH_2^+ = 29$ | $CH_3CO^+ = 43$ | $CH_3CH_2CO^+ = 57$ | $CH_3CH_2COCH_3^+ = 72$ peaks (fragments) in MS visible

Fragmentation reaction:

not visible in MS   43

-> Difference in Mass between Molecular Ion and fragment (**72 – 43 = 29**) indicates group lost (CH_3CH_2)
-> fragments, and difference between fragments, give information about the molecular structure & help with identification

Infrared spectroscopy

IR spectroscopy

-> To **identify** different types of covalent **bonds** => **functional groups**

-> **Identifying** a **molecule** by comparing pattern of **fingerprint region** ($1000 - 1550$ cm^{-1}) with known compound

- Absorption of IR radiation lets bond vibrate (different bonds – different frequency)
- Spectrum: transmittance (%) versus wavenumber (cm^{-1})
- transmittance: reverse of absorbance
- wavenumber: inverse of wavelength
- wavenumber: the smaller the less energy (C-C 990 cm^{-1}, C=C 1640 cm^{-1})
- Data Sheet with functional groups and wavenumbers is provided in exam

Other applications:
- accurate test for alcohol in breath of drunk drivers (evidence in law court)
  -> Ratio of OH-peak to CH peak of Ethanol
- to monitor air pollution (CO, NO, SO_2, CH_4)

Unit 3 – Investigative and Practical Skills

Accuracy and Reliability

Accuracy and Reliability

Accuracy: how close the result is to the true value

Reliability: How reproducible the result is

- The more times an experiment is repeated the more reliable the results become.
- This reduces effect of random errors (e.g. limitation of accuracy of pipette, 49.9 ml, 50.1 ml etc.)
- But the result can still be wrong due to a systematic error (e. g. wrong calibration of a balance -> always 0.5 g to heavy.

Percentage of Uncertainty

Percentage of Uncertainty

Definition: The uncertainty in a single measurement from a single instrument is **half the least count (unit) of the instrument**

-> add uncertainties of each instrument together

Example:
- burette with 0.1 ml graduation => +/- 0.05 ml (maximum error) -> 0.05 ml uncertainty
- two readings (before and after titration) two times uncertainty 2 x 0.05 ml = 0.1 ml total uncertainty for the titration
- Used 10 ml of standard solution for the titration (*titre*)
- Uncertainty: 0.1 ml/10 ml = 1.0 %

Acids

Acids

Definitions (Bronsted-Lowry):
Acid – proton (H^+) donor
Base – proton acceptor

Important acids:

HCl	hydrochloric acid (hydrogen chloride) – s
H_2SO_4	sulphuric acid - s
HNO_3	nitric acid - s
HNO_2	nitrous acid - w
H_2CO_3	carbonic acid - w
CH_3COOH	acetic acid, ethanoic acid - w
H_3PO_4	phosphoric acid - w

Acids reacting with metals forming hydrogen (Redox)

$Mg + H_2SO_4 -> MgSO_4 + H_2$

Strong acids (s):
Completely dissociated:
$HCl \quad -> \quad H^+ + Cl^-$

Weak acids (w):
Partially dissociated:
$CH_3COOH \rightleftarrows CH_3COO^- + H^+$
=> equilibrium

Bases

Bases

-> Proton (H^+) acceptor

Metal oxides
MgO + 2HCl -> $MgCl_2$ + H_2 Indigestion tablets

Hydroxides
$Ca(OH)_2$ + 2HCl -> $CaCl_2$ + $2H_2O$ Neutralises acid soils

Ammonia
NH_3 + HCl-> NH_4Cl Fertilizer

Carbonates
$CaCO_3$ + 2HCl -> $CaCl_2$ + H_2O + **CO_2**   **Fizzing -> acid test**

An **Alkali** is a soluble base (base that dissolves in water and releases OH^-)

Test for CO_2:
$Ca(OH)_{2\ (aq)}$ + $CO_{2\ (g)}$ > $CaCO_{3\ (s)}$ + $H_2O_{\ (l)}$
limewater turns milky (precipitation) in presence of CO_2

-> Anion of weak acid is a base (conjugated base)
*-> Anion of strong acid is **not** a base*

Acids and Bases preparation

Acids and Bases preparation

Acids:

Non-metal-oxide + H_2O -> Acid

CO_2 + H_2O -> H_2CO_3

-> Non-metal-oxides are hidden acids (*Lewis acid*)

Base:

Metaloxide + H_2O -> Metalhydroxide

CaO + H_2O -> $Ca(OH)_2$

-> Metal oxide are hidden hydroxides/bases (*Lewis base*)

$SO_2 + CaO -> CaSO_3$ (gas scrubbers: remove of SO_2)

Titrations

Titrations

-> method to determine a concentration

Acid-Base Titration (Neutralization)

Indicator *(weak organic acid)*
- indicates pH jump by colour change at endpoint
- pH range over which indicator changes colour is approximately two pH units ($pK_a(In)$ +/- 1)

phenolphthalein:	colourless (a)	-> pink (b)
methyl orange:	red (a)	-> yellow (b)
bromothymol blue:	yellow (a)	-> blue (b)
not universal indicator	-> too gradual colour change	

Endpoint, equivalence point (same number of moles of H^+ & OH^-)
-> pH of indicator colour change (pka) must match equivalence point:
- Weak base with strong acid -> methyl orange (pka = 3.5)
- Weak acid with strong base -> phenolphthalein (pka = 9.3)
- Strong acid with strong base -> any indicator

Titration Steps

Titration Steps

- clean burette by flushing with distilled H_2O and standard solution (water dilutes standard)
- fill burette with standard solution above 0 and drain to 0 mark (removes air bubbles in tap)
- fill exact volume of unknown solution, with volumetric pipette, in conical flask
- add few drops of indicator (too much indicator would change pH)
- use white tile as background
- do rough titration to get an idea for the endpoint
- do accurate titration and repeat at least three times (reliability)
- record volumes of standard solution used (eyes level, bottom of meniscus)
- calculate the average volume
- calculate moles of standard solution from volume using $n = c \, V$
- calculate concentration of unknown solution by using $c = n/V$

Accuracy of volume measurement

volumetric pipette > graduated pipette > burette > measuring cylinder

Preparing a Standard Solution

Preparing a Standard Solution

- calculate moles of compound from volume and concentration by using $n = c\ V$
- calculate mass of compound by using $m = n\ M$
- place a plastic weighing boat (dish) or weighing paper on a digital balance and zero the balance (tare)
- weigh the compound to an appropriate number of decimal places (e. g. 0.01)
- if the solid compound has been stored in the fridge allow it to reach room temperature before opening the bottle
- transfer the compound into a beaker which already contains some solvent (distilled H_2O) –> around 80 % of the final volume (e. g. 80 ml of 100 ml final volume)
- the solvent should be at room temperature
- rinse the weighing boat with distilled water to transfer the remaining compound, sticking to the boat, into the beaker
- dissolve by stirring the mixture, of compound and solvent, in the beaker
- if it's necessary to heat or cool to aid dissolving, ensure the solution has reached room temperature before the next step
- transfer the solution to a volumetric flask using a funnel
- rinse the beaker and stirrer and add the washing water into the flask
- slowly add distilled water up to the calibration mark of the flask (bottom of the meniscus)
- insert stopper and shake thoroughly to ensure complete mixing
- label the flask

Separating funnel

<u>Separating funnel</u>

-> To separate on organic phase from an aqueous phase

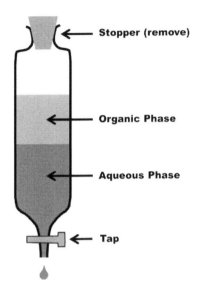

- During the synthesis of an organic compound, in an aqueous solution, the mixture is shaken for a prolonged amount of time in the separating funnel
- Pressure has to be released by opening the stopper frequently (product is volatile)
- Allow the mixture to stand and it will separate into two layers (organic phase & aqueous phase)
- The organic layer is usually on top, due to its lower density
- The aqueous layer contains impurities and can be drained by opening the stopper and the tap
- Close the tap when the organic layer reaches it
- Transfer the organic product into a storage bottle

Reflux apparatus

Reflux apparatus

-> To heat a reaction mixture with volatile liquids

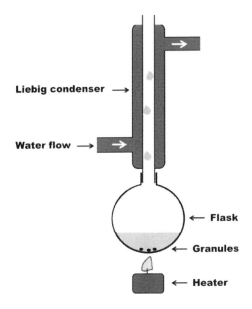

Liebig condenser →

Water flow →

← Flask

← Granules

← Heater

- Most organic reactions need heating for the reaction to happen
- Volatile reactants or products would evaporate and escape as gases
- The flask cannot be closed otherwise it would explode
- To prevent evaporation the gaseous compounds are condensed back into liquids, in the Liebig condenser
- These liquids drop back into the reaction flask
- Here they are collected (products) or continue to react (reactants)
- Anti-bumping granules smooth the boiling process

Distillation apparatus

Distillation apparatus

-> To separate different fractions of a mixture by boiling points

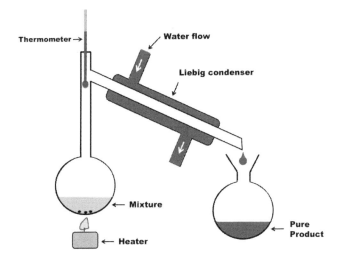

- After an organic reaction there is usually a mixture of products and unreacted reactants
- The desired product can be separated from the mixture at its boiling point by heating
- Compounds with lower boiling points evaporate first
- They condense in the Liebig-cooler and are collected
- The collection vessel is changed when the boiling point of the desired product is reached (indicated by the thermometer: the temperature remains constant for a while)
- This pure product is then collected and stored
- If the product still contains impurities it can be distilled again

Drying with anhydrous salts

Drying organic products

-> anhydrous salts are used to remove traces of water from an organic product

- After separation of an organic product from the reaction mixture, with a separating funnel or distillation, it might still contain traces of water
- These traces can be removed by adding solid anhydrous salts like $MgSO_4$ or $CaCl_2$
- The water gets incorporated into the salt crystal as water of crystallization
- The salt is then removed by filtration or decanting

14985026R00089

Printed in Great Britain
by Amazon.co.uk, Ltd.,
Marston Gate.